A Little Bit of
FOOTBALL
WIT

Tom Hay

summersdale

A LITTLE BIT OF FOOTBALL WIT

An Hachette UK Company
www.hachette.co.uk

Summersdale Publishers Ltd
Part of Octopus Publishing Group Limited
Carmelite House
50 Victoria Embankment
LONDON
EC4Y 0DZ
UK

www.summersdale.com

Printed and bound in Malta

ISBN: 978-1-78685-249-6

Substantial discounts on bulk quantities of Summersdale books are available to corporations, professional associations and other organisations. For details contact general enquiries: telephone: +44 (0) 1243 771107 or email: enquiries@summersdale.com.

CONTENTS

Editor's Note   5

Can You Manage it?   6

Ignorance Is Bliss   13

Whistle-stop Tours   19

A Blood Sport   25

A Safe Pair of Hands?   32

International Duty   39

Injury Time   47

Club Life   53

Strategic Skills   63

In a Manner of Speaking   70

Goals, Goals, Goals   80

A WAG's Tale   88

Unsavoury Comparisons   92

Born to Lose   100

Aiming Below the Belt   107

Make Your Mind Up   118

Winner Takes All   125

EDITOR'S NOTE

Football players aren't necessarily expected to be amusing, or even articulate. As Brian Clough once noted, 'their brains are in their feet'. Which means that when someone does come out with a thought-provoking comment, people often react as if they've just heard a latter-day Shakespeare.

However, a lot of the so-called wit in these pages is unwitting: confused (and often confusing) meanderings on lame duck managers, overpriced and under-performing stars, visually challenged referees and cash-hungry magnates. Whether intentional, accidental, or just plain nonsensical, this collection of riotous quips and quotes is sure to remind you that football is, and always will be, a funny old game.

CAN YOU MANAGE IT?

There's only one certainty in football: managers get sacked.

BRIAN KERR

Steve McClaren has achieved the unique feat of making even Sven Goran-Eriksson look good.

IAN RIDLEY ON McCLAREN'S BRIEF SPELL AS MANAGER OF ENGLAND

Barry Fry's management is
based on the chaos theory.

MARK McGHEE

Alex Ferguson is the best
manager I've had at this level.
Well, he's the only manager
I've had at this level.

DAVID BECKHAM

CHELSEA HAVE JUST LAUNCHED A NEW AFTERSHAVE CALLED 'THE SPECIAL ONE' BY U GO BOSS.

Pat Flanagan after José Mourinho's shock departure from Chelsea in September 2007

MICK McCARTHY BREAKS INTO A RASH IF HE'S WITHIN 30 YARDS OF AN NUJ CARD.

Tom Humphries

The secret... is to keep the six players who hate you away from the five who are undecided.

JOCK STEIN ON HOW TO BE A GOOD MANAGER

I have come to the conclusion that nice men do not make the best managers.

GRAEME SOUNESS

IGNORANCE
IS BLISS

DAN QUAYLE THINKS THE GAZA STRIP IS PAUL GASCOIGNE'S FOOTBALL JERSEY.

Johnny Carson

An oxymoron is when
two contradictory concepts
are juxtaposed, as in
'footballing brain'.

PATRICK MURRAY

He's got the brains of
a rocking horse.

DAVE BASSETT ON SHEFFIELD UNITED
GOALKEEPER SIMON TRACEY

JASON ROBERTS? THIS IS A MAN WHO SPELT HIS NAME WRONG ON HIS TRANSFER REQUEST.

Gary Megson

Paul Gascoigne wore a number ten jersey. I thought that was his position, but it turned out it was his IQ.

GEORGE BEST

Well, I can play in the centre, on the right, and occasionally on the left-hand side.

DAVID BECKHAM WHEN ASKED IF IT WOULD BE FAIR TO DESCRIBE HIM AS A VOLATILE PLAYER

WHISTLE-STOP TOURS

FOOTBALL IS A GAME WITH 22 PLAYERS, TWO LINESMEN AND 20,000 REFEREES.

Bob Monkhouse

I used to play football in my youth but then my eyes went bad so I became a referee.

ERIC MORECAMBE

I never comment on referees and I'm not going to break the habit of a lifetime for that prat.

RON ATKINSON

I'VE SEEN HARDER TACKLES IN THE PIE QUEUE AT HALF-TIME THAN THE ONES PUNISHED IN GAMES.

George Fulston on overly strict referees

The referee was booking so many people I thought he was filling in his lottery numbers.

IAN WRIGHT

The trouble with referees is that they just don't care which side wins.

TOM CANTERBURY

A BLOOD
SPORT

I'M NOT HAPPY WITH OUR TACKLING, BOYS. WE KEEP HURTING THEM, BUT THEY KEEP GETTING UP.

Jimmy Murphy

They say the new striker I'm marking is fast. Maybe, but how fast can he limp?

MICK McCARTHY

The Liverpool theme song is 'You'll Never Walk Alone'. The Wimbledon one is 'You'll Never Walk Again'.

TOMMY DOCHERTY

IT'S NOT FAIR TO SAY THAT LEE BOWYER IS RACIST; HE'D STAMP ON ANYONE'S HEAD.

Rodney Marsh

Get your retaliation in first.

ALASTAIR DUNN

In football it is widely
acknowledged that if both
sides agree to cheat, then
cheating is fair.

C. B. FRY

IF HE FOULS YOU HE NORMALLY PICKS YOU UP, BUT THE REFEREE DOESN'T SEE WHAT HE PICKS YOU UP BY.

Ryan Giggs on Dennis Wise

A SAFE
PAIR OF
HANDS?

You have to remember that
a goalkeeper is a goalkeeper
because he can't play football.

RUUD GULLIT

He hasn't made any saves
you wouldn't have expected
him not to make.

LIAM BRADY

POOR SCOTT CARSON. JUST TWO MORE HANDS AND ANOTHER CHEST AND HE WOULD HAVE SAVED IT.

Jimmy Greaves on one of the goals
that put England out of Euro 2008

Neville Southall was a big daft goalie... he once turned up at Wembley wearing his suit and a pair of flip-flops.

ANDY GRAY

David Icke says he's here to save the world. Well he saved bugger all... in goal for Coventry.

JASPER CARROTT

THAT WOULD HAVE BEEN A GOAL IF THE GOALKEEPER HADN'T SAVED IT.

Kevin Keegan

The most vulnerable area for
goalies is between their legs.

ANDY GRAY

It's not nice going into the
supermarket and the woman at
the till is thinking 'dodgy keeper'.

DAVID JAMES

INTERNATIONAL DUTY

THE CROATIANS DON'T PLAY WELL WITHOUT THE BALL.

Barry Venison

I've just named the team I would like to represent Wales in the next World Cup: Brazil.

BOBBY GOULD

The English football team – brilliant on paper, shit on grass.

ARTHUR SMITH

OTHER NATIONS HAVE HISTORY. WE HAVE FOOTBALL.

Ondino Viera

SCOTLAND HAS THE ONLY FOOTBALL TEAM IN THE WORLD THAT DOES A LAP OF DISGRACE.

Billy Connolly

San Marino play like men
who expect to encounter visa
problems if they approach
the halfway line.

TOM HUMPHRIES

To play Holland you have
to play the Dutch.

RUUD GULLIT

If you have a fortnight's holiday
in Dublin you qualify to play for
the national side.

MIKE ENGLAND

1966 was a great year for English
football. Eric Cantona was born.

ANONYMOUS

INJURY
TIME

MY ANKLE WAS POINTING TOWARDS HONG KONG SO I KNEW I WAS IN TROUBLE.

Alan Smith after breaking his leg in 2006

Leeds United are having problems with injuries. The players keep recovering.

BILL SHANKLY AT A TIME WHEN LEEDS WERE HAVING A BAD RUN

★ ★ ★ ★ ★ ★ ★

John Barnes' problem is that he gets injured appearing on *A Question of Sport.*

TOMMY DOCHERTY

I WAS WATCHING GERMANY AND… GOT UP TO MAKE A CUP OF TEA. I BUMPED INTO THE TELLY AND KLINSMANN FELL OVER.

Frank Skinner

He's had two cruciates and a broken ankle. That's not easy. Every player... is praying the boy gets a break.

ALEX FERGUSON ON WES BROWN

When England go to Turkey there could be fatalities. Or even worse, injuries.

PHIL NEAL

CLUB
LIFE

WHEN I WAS PLAYING FOR MANCHESTER UNITED I USED TO GO MISSING A LOT: MISS AMERICA, MISS URUGUAY, MISS PERU...

George Best

All Nottingham has is Robin Hood.
And he's dead.

**BRYAN ROY AFTER HE LEFT
NOTTINGHAM FOREST**

The problems at Wimbledon seem
to be that the club has suffered a
loss of complacency.

JOE KINNEAR

THE TWO BEST CLUBS IN LONDON ARE STRINGFELLOWS AND THE HIPPODROME.

Terry McDermott

As a small boy I was torn between
two ambitions: to be a footballer
or to run away and join a circus.
At Partick Thistle I got to do both.

ALAN HANSEN

If Everton were playing down
at the bottom of my garden,
I'd draw the curtains.

BILL SHANKLY

SOUTHAMPTON IS A VERY WELL RUN FOOTBALL TEAM FROM MONDAY TO FRIDAY. IT'S SATURDAYS WE HAVE A PROBLEM WITH.

Lawrie McMenemy

WATCHING MANCHESTER CITY IS PROBABLY THE BEST LAXATIVE YOU CAN TAKE.

Phil Neal

A contract on... paper,
saying you want to leave, is
like a piece of paper saying
you want to leave.

JOHN HOLLINS

I'd like to play for an Italian club,
like Barcelona.

MARK DRAPER

STRATEGIC
SKILLS

ALLY McLEOD THINKS TACTICS ARE A NEW KIND OF PEPPERMINT.

Simon Douglas

All I used to say was, 'Whenever possible, pass the ball to George.'

MATT BUSBY ON GEORGE BEST

If there's an effective way to kill off the threat of Maradona... it probably involves... tethering him to a stake in front of a firing squad.

HUGH McILVANNEY

IF YOU PLAYED FOOTBALL ON A BLACKBOARD, DON HOWE WOULD WIN THE WORLD CUP EVERY TIME.

Willie Johnston

Football isn't just about playing well. It's about making the other team play not so well.

ROY PAUL

Fail to prepare; prepare to fail.

ROY KEANE

It's easy to beat Brazil. You just stop them getting within 20 yards of your goal.

BOBBY CHARLTON

Anyone who uses the word 'quintessentially' in a half-time team talk is talking crap.

MICK McCARTHY

IN A
MANNER OF
SPEAKING

If you don't like the heat in
the dressing room, get out
of the kitchen.

TERRY VENABLES

Graeme Souness went
behind my back right
in front of my face.

CRAIG BELLAMY

WE CAN ONLY COME OUT OF THIS GAME WITH EGG ON OUR FACES, SO IT'S A REAL BANANA SKIN.

Ray Stewart before a crunch tie in the Scottish Cup in 2001

Not being in the Rumbelows
Cup for those teams won't mean
a row of beans, cos that's only
small potatoes.

IAN ST JOHN

Manchester United have got the
bull between the horns now.

BILLY McNEILL

THOSE ARE THE SORT OF DOORS THAT GET OPENED IF YOU DON'T CLOSE THEM.

Terry Venables

SOMETIMES YOU OPEN YOUR MOUTH AND IT PUNCHES YOU STRAIGHT BETWEEN THE EYES.

Ian Rush

We could be putting the hammer
in Luton's coffin.

RAY WILKINS

And tonight we have the added
ingredient of Kenny Dalglish
not being here.

MARTIN TYLER

THE GROIN'S A LITTLE SORE BUT AFTER THE SEMI-FINAL I PUT IT TO THE BACK OF MY HEAD.

Michael Hughes

GOALS, GOALS, GOALS

Norman Whiteside was more a scorer of great goals than a great scorer of goals.

PAUL McGRATH

The best thing for them to do is stay at nil–nil until they score a goal.

MARTIN O'NEILL

IT WAS THE SORT OF GOAL THAT MADE YOUR HAIR STAND UP ON YOUR SHOULDERS.

Niall Quinn

Two hundred league goals in
one season… last I heard of him
he was working somewhere
on a building site.

GEORGE BEST ON RON DAVIES IN 1982

Apart from their goals,
Norway haven't scored.

TERRY VENABLES

OUR PROBLEM IS THAT WE'VE TRIED TO SCORE TOO MANY GOALS.

Gordon Lee

The fools.
They've scored too early.

**EAMONN SWEENEY ON A 1998 GAME
OF GAELIC FOOTBALL DURING WHICH SLIGO
SCORED FIRST AND THEN LOST**

Woodcock would have scored
there but his shot was just
too perfect.

RON ATKINSON

After I scored six against
Northampton I hung back...
I didn't want to score any more.
It was getting embarrassing.

GEORGE BEST

David Batty is quite prolific, isn't
he? He scores one goal a season,
regular as clockwork.

KENNY DALGLISH

A WAG'S TALE

I've read David's autobiography from cover to cover. It's got some nice pictures.

VICTORIA BECKHAM

My plan was to chill out for a few years and spend time with my family but they got fed up with me. My wife dropped me off at the stadium.

ROY KEANE ON HIS INTENTIONS TO RELAX AFTER HIS PLAYING CAREER ENDED

He talked about nothing but football. By the time I left him, I knew more about it than most managers.

DANIELLE SOUNESS, ON HER EX-HUSBAND, GRAEME

She Tarzan, he Jane.

ANDREW MORTON ON THE RELATIONSHIP BETWEEN POSH AND BECKS

THE WOMAN SITS, GETTING COLDER AND COLDER, ON A SEAT GETTING HARDER AND HARDER, WATCHING OAFS GETTING MUDDIER AND MUDDIER.

Virginia Graham

UNSAVOURY COMPARISONS

Steve Staunton's honeymoon as manager of Ireland lasted about as long as one of Britney Spears' marriages.

KEVIN PALMER

If you're a sports channel that doesn't have football, you're effectively shovelling water with a sieve.

ANDY GRAY

Trevor Brooking floats like
a butterfly – and stings
like one as well.

BRIAN CLOUGH

Davor Šuker has a first
touch like a camel.

RON ATKINSON

DUNCAN MacKENZIE IS LIKE A BEAUTIFUL MOTOR CAR – SIX OWNERS, BUT HE'S BEEN IN THE GARAGE MOST OF THE TIME.

John Toshack

A MAN'S SEXUAL FANTASY IS TWO LESBIANS AND A DONKEY MAKING OUT TO THE MUSIC OF *MATCH OF THE DAY*.

Jo Brand

What is it that Rangers, Celtic and a three-pin plug have in common? They're all completely useless in Europe.

MICHAEL MUNRO

Vinnie Jones is to fair football what Count Dracula was to blood transfusions.

MICHAEL HERD

OWEN, ONCE THE BABY-FACED ASSASSIN, HAS HAD TO MAKE WAY FOR ROONEY, THE ASSASSIN-FACED BABY.

Daniel Taylor

BORN TO
LOSE

Those who tell you it's tough
at the top have never been
at the bottom.

JOE HARVEY

In 1978, in between Manchester
City winning two games in
succession, there had
been three Popes.

FRANK SKINNER

For years I thought the club's name was Partick Thistle Nil.

BILLY CONNOLLY

We don't use a stopwatch to judge our Golden Goal competition now; we use a calendar.

TOMMY DOCHERTY ON THE STANDARD OF PLAY AT WOLVES IN 1985

WE'VE GOT A LONG-TERM PLAN AT THIS CLUB AND EXCEPT FOR THE RESULTS IT'S GOING WELL.

Chairman of Fulham FC

THE STANDARD OF SWEET TROLLEYS AT THE TEAM GET-TOGETHERS.

Pat Nevin after being asked what was the greatest improvement in Scottish football in the past ten years

A lot of hard work went
into this defeat.

MALCOLM ALLISON

My doctor told me I should avoid
any excitement, so I've started
watching Millwall.

LES DAWSON

AIMING
BELOW
THE BELT

GORDON STRACHAN'S TONGUE CAN KILL A MAN AT TEN PACES.

Mick Hennigan

When Frank Stapleton wakes up... he rushes to the mirror and smiles, just to get it over with.

TONY CASCARINO

Eric Cantona couldn't tackle a fish supper.

ALEX FERGUSON

ALAN SHEARER IS BORING; WE CALL HIM MARY POPPINS.

Freddy Shepherd, who later apologised for insulting Mary Poppins

DALGLISH WASN'T... BIG BUT HE HAD A HUGE ARSE THAT CAME DOWN BELOW HIS KNEES. THAT'S WHERE HE GOT HIS STRENGTH FROM.

Brian Clough

Carlton covers every blade
of grass on the pitch, but then
you have to if your first
touch is that crap.

DAVE JONES ON CARLTON PALMER

Just when you thought there
were no surprises left in football,
Vinnie Jones turns out to be an
international player.

JIMMY GREAVES

BECKHAM CAN'T KICK WITH HIS LEFT FOOT... CAN'T HEAD A BALL AND HE CAN'T TACKLE. APART FROM THAT HE'S ALL RIGHT.

George Best

WHY DO ARSENAL FANS SMELL? SO THE BLIND CAN HATE THEM AS WELL.

Joe Lynam

MAKE YOUR MIND UP

When I said they'd scored two goals what I meant, of course, was that they only scored one.

GEORGE HAMILTON

We're on the crest of a slump.

JACK CHARLTON

For those of you watching in black and white, Spurs are in the all-yellow strip.

JOHN MOTSON

You can't guarantee anything in football. All you can guarantee is disappointment.

GRAEME SOUNESS

CERTAIN PEOPLE ARE FOR ME, CERTAIN PEOPLE ARE PRO ME.

Terry Venables

WITH THE VERY LAST KICK OF THE GAME, MacDONALD SCORED WITH A HEADER.

Alan Parry

They're still in the game, and
they're trying to get back into it.

JIMMY HILL

If Glenn Hoddle said one word
to his team at half-time, it was
'concentration' and 'focus'.

RON ATKINSON

WINNER
TAKES ALL

We got the winner three
minutes from time, but then
they equalised.

IAN McNAIL

Not to win is guttering.

MARK NOBLE

For a few minutes it looked like Wigan would win, but then the game started.

KEN RONAN

We lost because we didn't win.

RONALDO

If you're interested in finding out more about our books, find us on Facebook at **Summersdale Publishers** and follow us on Twitter at **@Summersdale**.

www.summersdale.com